Where in the World Can I . . .

FIND A DRAGON?

Where in the World Can I . . .

FIND A DRAGON?

www.worldbook.com

World Book, Inc.
180 North LaSalle Street, Suite 900
Chicago, Illinois 60601
USA

For information about other World Book publications, visit our website at **www.worldbook.com** or call **1-800-WORLDBK (967-5325).**

For information about sales to schools and libraries, call 1-800-975-3250 (United States), or 1-800-837-5365 (Canada).

Library of Congress Cataloging-in-Publication Data for this volume has been applied for.

Where in the World Can I…
ISBN: 978-0-7166-2178-2 (set, hc.)

Find a Dragon?
ISBN: 978-0-7166-2182-9 (hc.)

Also available as:
ISBN: 978-0-7166-2192-8 (e-book)

1st printing July 2018

STAFF

Writer: Shawn Brennan

Executive Committee
President
Jim O'Rourke

Vice President and Editor in Chief
Paul A. Kobasa

Vice President, Finance
Donald D. Keller

Vice President, Marketing
Jean Lin

Vice President, International Sales
Maksim Rutenberg

Vice President, Technology
Jason Dole

Director, Human Resources
Bev Ecker

Editorial
Director, New Print
Tom Evans

Managing Editor, New Print
Jeff De La Rosa

Senior Editor, New Print
Shawn Brennan

Editor, New Print
Grace Guibert

Librarian
S. Thomas Richardson

Manager, Contracts & Compliance (Rights & Permissions)
Loranne K. Shields

Manager, Indexing Services
David Pofelski

Digital
Director, Digital Produ
Development
Erika Meller

Manager, Digital Prod
Jonathan Wills

Graphics and Design
Senior Art Director
Tom Evans

Coordinator, Design Development and Production
Brenda Tropinski

Media Researcher
Rosalia Bledsoe

Manufacturing/ Production
Manufacturing Manag
Anne Fritzinger

Proofreader
Nathalie Strassheim

TABLE OF CONTENTS

WHAT IS A DRAGON?

A dragon is a beast found in the *legends* (old stories) of Europe and Asia. The legends tell that dragons are big creatures. They breathe fire and have a long, scaly tail like a lizard's. Many of them have wings and can fly.

In tales from Europe, dragons are usually fierce and evil. But Asian dragons are often friendly and bring good luck and wealth.

Many of the European legends tell how a hero kills a dragon. A story about Apollo, a god of the ancient Greeks and Romans, tells that he once killed a dragon called Python. These stories seem to be about frightening things in the world that people try to overcome.

Saint George rescued a princess from a dragon by killing the beast with a spear. Saint George is the patron saint of England. A *saint* is a holy person who becomes a religious hero by being especially good. A *patron saint* protects a place or group of people.

Some legends tell that dragons lived in wild, far-away places. The dragons guarded treasures in their dens. A person who killed a dragon won the dragon's treasure.

Sigurd *(SIHG urd)* the Dragon Slayer was the most famous *Norse* (ancient Scandinavian) hero. He killed Fafnir (*FAHV nir)*, a powerful, greedy man who turned himself into a dragon to guard the gold he stole from his own family.

Beowulf *(BAY uh wulf)* died in a fight with a dragon that breathed fire to guard its treasure. Beowulf is a character in an old English epic. An *epic* is a long poem that tells a story. Beowulf fights and wins against other monsters before his last fight with the dragon.

The dragons in the legends of China and Japan and other countries in Asia are welcome creatures. One old Chinese belief is that certain dragons can make the rainfall that is needed to produce a good harvest.

In China and in Chinese communities around the world, Chinese New Year is celebrated with a parade. The parade almost always includes a group of people that winds through the street wearing a large dragon costume.

It is an old Chinese belief that the dragon stops evil spirits from spoiling the new year.

Since ancient times, people have also told tales of creatures called sea serpents. A *serpent* is a big snake. These sea serpents look like dragons, but they live in water. Many legends of Asia tell about dragons that look like serpents and live beneath the sea. These dragons cause storms. The Bible includes a story about Leviathan *(luh VY uh thuhn)*, a giant sea serpent.

In our own time, some people say they have seen sea serpents. The people say they see a line of dark humps just above the waves. Some people believe that a sea serpent lives in Loch *(lok)* Ness. Loch Ness is a lake in northern Scotland. For many years, researchers have explored the lake. So far, there is no proof that the Loch Ness monster is real.

The idea of dragons still thrills people today. Popular books and games have featured dragons. Many movies have been made about ancient and modern dragons. Even though dragons are make-believe beasts, you might see some living animals that look very much like dragons! Read on to find out where!

DUNGEONS & DRAGONS

KOMODO NATIONAL PARK—HOME TO DRAGONS

Real, live dragons live at Komodo *(kuh MOH doh)* National Park. The park is in the Southeast Asian island country of Indonesia. This real, live dragon is called a Komodo dragon! The Komodo dragon is the world's largest living lizard. A lizard belongs to the group of animals called *reptiles.* Snakes belong to this family, too.

The government of Indonesia set up Komodo National Park in 1980. The dragons live on only a few islands. The government turned those islands into the park to make a safe place for the Komodo dragons. Even these fierce animals need help to survive as more people fill the world.

Hundreds of dragons live in the park. You can trek along with a park ranger to see some of them! A *ranger* is a person who helps to keep wild areas and the animals that live in them safe. The rangers help people to enjoy visiting the areas and seeing the animals. But these animals are very dangerous. You should not walk in the park without a ranger. We must give the dragons and all wild animals their space.

The park also is a safe place for plants and other animals that live there. In 1991, the United Nations Educational, Scientific and Cultural Organization (UNESCO) made the park a World Heritage Site. Some of these places are special because of the plants and animals that live there. Others are special because of events in history that happened at them. Governments are required to preserve and protect World Heritage Sites.

Now, let's learn about those dragons!

KOMODO DRAGON

The Komodo dragon grows to more than 10 feet (3 meters) long. A grown-up dragon can weigh as much as 365 pounds (165 kilograms). This giant lizard has a scaly body. Its head is long and flat, and its neck is long. There are sharp teeth in its mouth. It has short legs that are *bowed,* which means they bend out. The toes on its feet end in big claws. It has a strong tail.

When a Komodo dragon is cornered, it stands high on its legs and puffs up its body. This makes the dragon look even larger than it is. It will also hiss and open its mouth as wide as it can. The dragon may also use its tail like a whip or bite with its sharp teeth.

Komodo dragons make venom *(VEHN uhm)*, or poison, in their mouth. When a dragon bites an animal, the venom can stop the animal from moving. It even can kill the animal. Either way, it makes it easier for the dragon to catch and eat the animal.

Komodo dragons often eat the meat that they scavenge *(SKAV uhnj)*. Scavengers look for and eat dead animals. A komodo dragon can smell with its long forked tongue! It can smell a dead animal several miles or kilometers away!

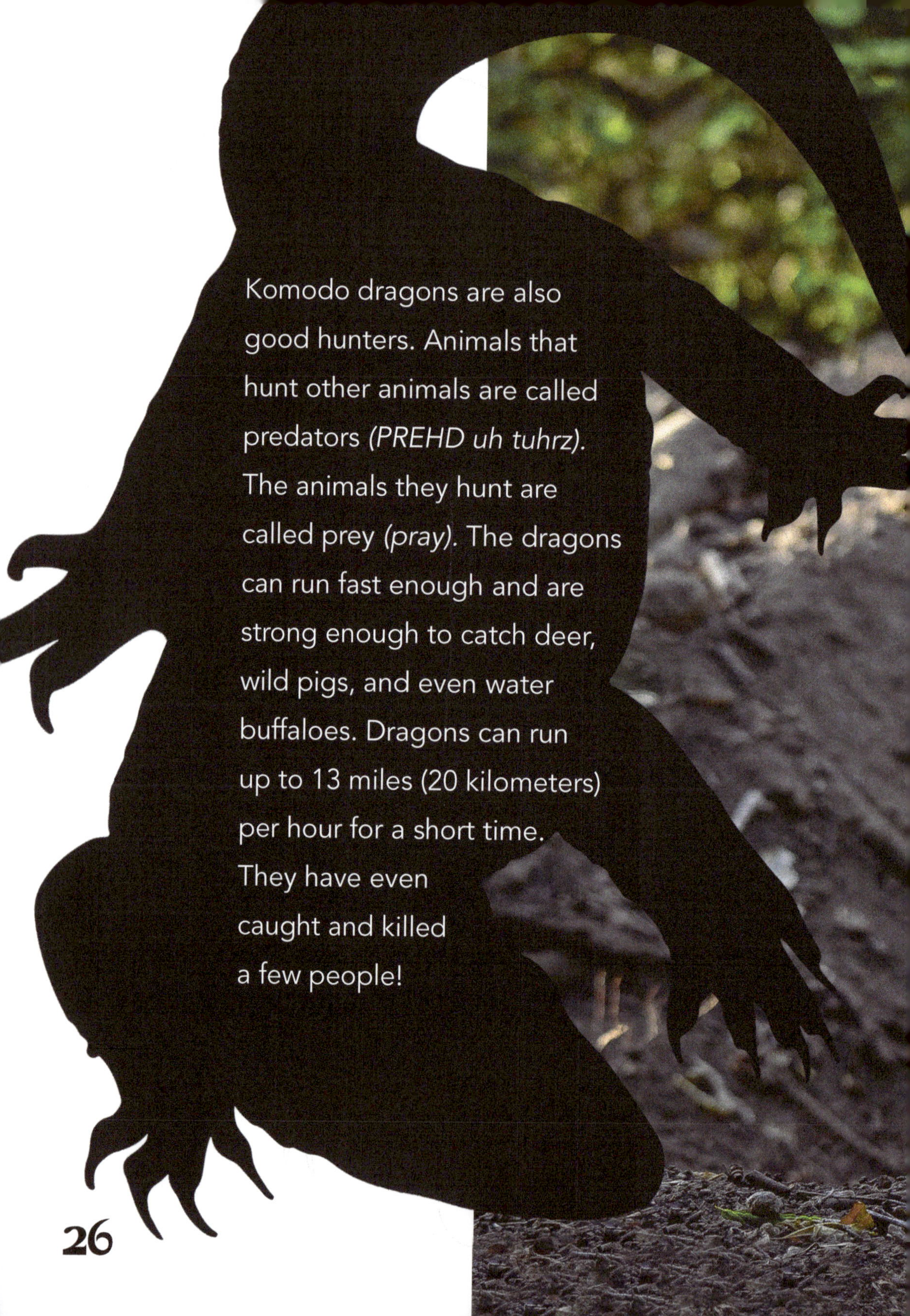

Komodo dragons are also good hunters. Animals that hunt other animals are called predators *(PREHD uh tuhrz).* The animals they hunt are called prey *(pray).* The dragons can run fast enough and are strong enough to catch deer, wild pigs, and even water buffaloes. Dragons can run up to 13 miles (20 kilometers) per hour for a short time. They have even caught and killed a few people!

The bite of a Komodo dragon badly hurts its prey. The prey may not be killed right away by the bite. The dragon may follow its prey for days until the wounded animal gets weak and falls.

A mother Komodo dragon digs a hole in which to lay her eggs. She may also take over a nest left behind by another animal. The mother Komodo dragon usually lays 15 to 30 eggs in the nest. The eggs hatch in eight to nine months. The baby Komodos are full grown at about five years. Komodo dragons can live for 50 years.

Komodo dragons are endangered because people destroy the lizards' *habitat,* the area where they live. People also have killed off many of the animals the Komodos hunt. *Endangered* animals are animals that could die out and be gone forever. People also trap dragons to sell them as pets.

People also kill the dragons. They hunt the dragons for their skin. People use the skins to make bags or wallets. Indonesia protects Komodo dragons from poachers. *Poaching* is hunting that is against the law. Biologists and other scientists are trying to save the dragons' habitat. Many zoos have set up dragon breeding programs. This helps the parents make more healthy babies that live.

MONITORS

The Komodo dragon is part of a large group of lizards called *monitors (MON uh tuhrz).* Other monitors live in the Solomon Islands, New Guinea, Australia, the East Indies, southern Asia, and Africa. In Australia, monitors are called *goannas (goh AN uhz).*

The Komodo dragon is the largest type of monitor. Other monitors are smaller. Most monitors are usually at least 4 feet (1.2 meters) long. Some grow to be 6 to 7 feet (1.8 to 2.1 meters) in length. Other well-known *species (SPEE sheez)*, or kinds, of monitors are the Nile monitor of Africa and the water monitor. The water monitor lives from India to northern Australia.

OTHER "DRAGONS"

FLYING DRAGON

Look up in the sky! It's a flying dragon! A flying dragon is a type of lizard. Flying dragons do not fly as birds fly. Rather, they glide through the air like a paper airplane. The lizard glides by spreading out folds of skin to form "wings." These "wings" act like a sail. They help to keep the animal in the air as it leaps from tree to tree.

When a flying dragon lands on a tree, it folds its wings and they become almost invisible. When the animal is ready to glide, it stretches out its wings again. A flying dragon also has small throat flaps, called *lappets*, that help with gliding. It uses its long tail to help steer. Some flying dragons can glide as far as 200 feet (60 meters) or more!

There are several dozen species of flying dragons. They live in tropical rain forests in southwestern India and all over Southeast Asia. There are a lot of flying dragon species in the Philippines and on the Sunda Shelf (Borneo, Sumatra, and the Malay Peninsula). They spend most of their time on the trunks of large trees, where they eat ants and termites. Flying dragons have slim bodies. The longest species measures about 15 inches (38 centimeters), including the tail.

Male flying dragons set up areas of their own. Some other animals do this, too. These areas are called *territories.* One dragon's territory may be made up of one to several trees. One dragon will often chase another one through the air, to keep the other dragon out of his territory.

A male also shows off its colorful wings, throat lappets, and *dewlap* (a triangular flap of skin below the chin) to keep others away. Males also show off to find a mate. The female flying dragon lays 1 to 4 eggs that she buries in the soil.

BEARDED DRAGON

The bearded dragon is a lizard that lives in Australia. This dragon has a *pouch* (small bag) of skin on its throat. The lizard can blow up its throat pouch with air. The pouch is covered in spiky scales that stick out when the pouch is full of air. This makes it look like the lizard has a beard and gives the dragon its name. There are several species of bearded dragons. They live in dry woodlands and rocky deserts. The lizards are popular pets, especially the species called the central bearded dragon.

Bearded dragons have rounded heads shaped like an arrow. They have spikes along their sides. Bearded dragons grow 1 to 2 feet (30 to 60 centimeters) long. Males are larger than females.

The coloring of bearded dragons matches the soil where they live. The coloring ranges from tan to brown to gold to red. They can lighten or darken the color of their skin in only a few minutes. Dragons can control how warm or cool their body is by changing their skin color and behavior. They turn their skin darker and flatten their bodies to get warm in the sun. They turn their skin lighter and climb bushes or dig into the ground to cool off.

Bearded dragons make movements to send messages. When one of these dragons is afraid, it blows up its throat pouch and turns the pouch skin dark. A dragon raises a front leg and waves it in circles to tell another dragon not to be afraid. Other dragon signals are moving the head up and down, opening the mouth wide, and moving the tail from side to side.

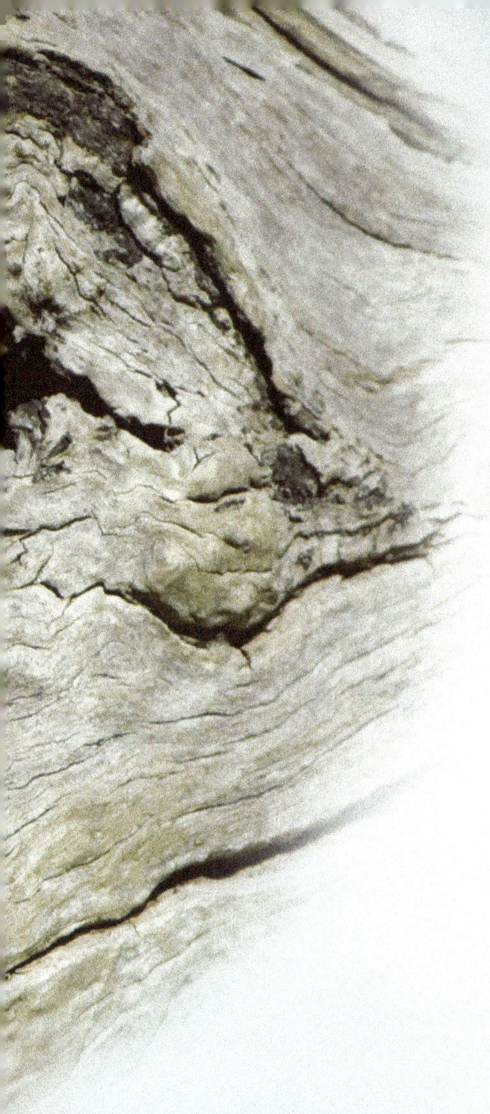

Bearded dragons eat both animals and plants. They hunt mostly insects and other small animals. Bearded dragons are eaten mainly by other lizards, snakes, and *birds of prey.* Birds of prey are large birds that hunt other animals. Female bearded dragons lay as many as 24 eggs in a *burrow* (hole) in the ground, up to nine times a year. The eggs hatch in 50 to 70 days. Bearded dragons live for up to 15 years.

SEADRAGON

A seadragon looks a bit like a small sea serpent! The seadragon is a type of fish that is like a seahorse. Like seahorses, seadragons have a long *snout* (nose) and skin covered in flat, bony pieces. But seadragons generally grow larger than seahorses. Seadragons have flatter bodies. Pieces of skin in different shapes grow out from their bodies.

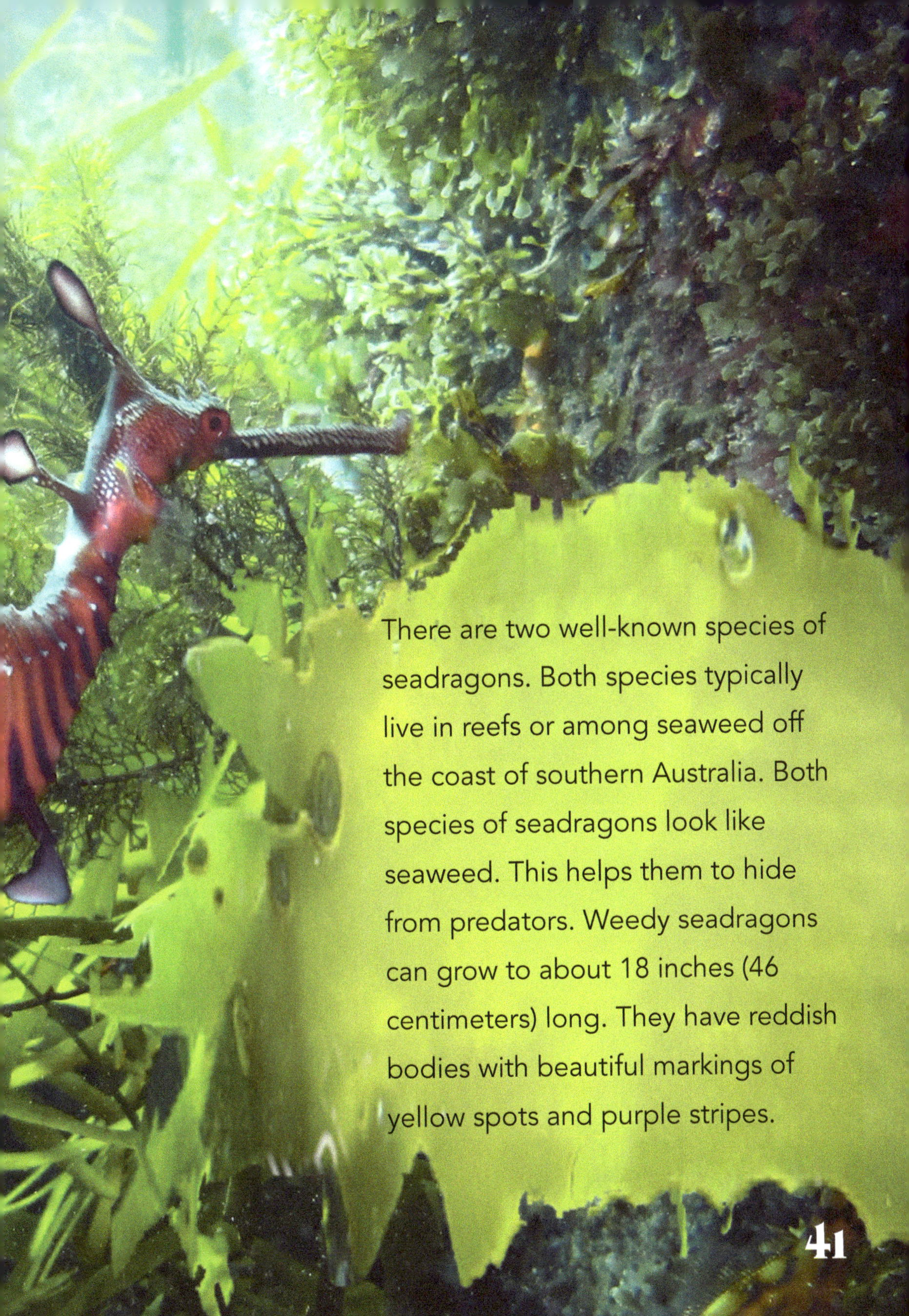

There are two well-known species of seadragons. Both species typically live in reefs or among seaweed off the coast of southern Australia. Both species of seadragons look like seaweed. This helps them to hide from predators. Weedy seadragons can grow to about 18 inches (46 centimeters) long. They have reddish bodies with beautiful markings of yellow spots and purple stripes.

Leafy seadragons are smaller. They have green or brownish-yellow bodies with purple and white stripes. They have flaps of skin on their bodies in the shapes of leaves. These flaps of skin are much larger than the ones on weedy seadragons. Leafy seadragons also have sharp spines on their sides. They may use these spines to fight off predators.

Seadragons are slow swimmers. They eat tiny living things called *zooplankton (ZOH uh PLANGK tuhn)* and other small swimming animals.

The dragons suck up the animals using their mouths like a drinking straw!

A female seadragon makes up to 300 eggs. The male takes care of the eggs by carrying them on the underside of his tail. Before it is time for him to carry the eggs, the male's tail gets bigger. Little holes form on the tail. The eggs will go into the holes. The eggs hatch in four to nine weeks. Seadragons can live for 10 years or more in an aquarium, but probably fewer in the wild.

FACE TO FACE WITH DRAGONS

If you can't make a trip to Komodo National Park in Indonesia, you can meet Komodo dragons at more than 50 zoos and aquariums around the world. Many species of monitors live in more than 300 zoos and aquariums. You can also see bearded dragons at many zoos. Also, some types of monitors, flying dragons, and bearded dragons are favorite pets for some people.

The government of Australia has worked to protect seadragons and has made it against the law to collect some types. But you can see seadragons in several aquariums around the world.

Whether you see a dragon in the wild or in a zoo, aquarium, or cage, be careful around the animal. Do not harm the area where the animal lives. The survival of these dragons depends on us!

BOOKS AND WEBSITES

BOOKS

Dragons by John Hamilton (ABDO, 2004)
This full-color book explores dragons of fantasy and folklore and places them in historical context.

Dragons by Stephen Krensky (Lerner, 2006)
This book examines the origin of the dragon in folklore and mythology and its rise to popularity as a media icon of today.

Dragons by Carla Mooney (ABDO, 2014)
Learn where and why legends of dragons began, how these creatures are reflected in different cultures, and how they are understood today. Includes primary sources with accompanying questions, charts, graphs, diagrams, timelines, and maps.

Venomous: How Earth's Deadliest Creatures Mastered Biochemistry by Christie Wilcox (Scientific American, 2016)
This book is an engrossing survey of the planet's venomous animals, including the Komodo dragon.

WEBSITES

Draconika Dragons
http://www.draconika.com/
Website on the history and cultural importance of dragons, as well as information on dragons in fantasy role-playing.

Komodo National Park
http://www.komodonationalpark.org/
Park's official website, maintained by the Indonesian Park authority and the Nature Conservancy. Includes information on the park, conservation efforts, an interactive map, and a photo gallery.

Komodo National Park - UNESCO World Heritage Centre
http://whc.unesco.org/en/list/609
UNESCO site on Komodo National Park. Includes information on conservation efforts, maps, photos, videos, and advisory body documents and reports.

INDEX

ACKNOWLEDGMENTS

Cover: © Josep Ng, Shutterstock; © DM7/Shutterstock; © Denis Andricic, Shutterstock

2-7 © Shutterstock

8-9 © Shutterstock; © Lebrecht Music and Arts Photo Library/Alamy Images

10-15 © Shutterstock

16-17 © Shutterstock; Toho; © Dungeons & Dragons

18-19 © Shutterstock

20-21 © Jeremy Brown, Dreamstime; © Shutterstock

22-23 © Gudkov Andrey, Shutterstock

24-25 © Shutterstock; © AY Images/iStockphoto

26-27 © Mbrand85/Shutterstock; © Vector Silhouettes/iStockphoto

28-29 © Mote Stock Photo/Shutterstock; © Michael Pitts, Minden Pictures; © Amsis1/Dreamstime

30-31 © Paul Morton, iStockphoto; © Five Spots/Shutterstock

32-33 © Chien Lee, Minden Pictures

34-41 © Shutterstock

42-43 © Michael Warwick, Shutterstock; © Zcello/Dreamstime

44-45 © Michael Shake, Shutterstock

www.ingramcontent.com/pod-product-compliance
Ingram Content Group UK Ltd.
Pitfield, Milton Keynes, MK11 3LW, UK
UKHW061951290726
14090UKWH00021B/1182

9 780716 65093